Music for Ghosts

Music for Ghosts

Christopher Locke

NQ Books™

The New York Quarterly Foundation, Inc.
Beacon, New York

NYQ Books™ is an imprint of The New York Quarterly Foundation, Inc.

The New York Quarterly Foundation, Inc.
P. O. Box 470
Beacon, NY 12508

www.nyq.org

First Edition

Set in New Baskerville

Layout and Design by Raymond P. Hammond

Cover Photo: "Vanishing Misguided Ghosts" by micjan / photoscase.com

Library of Congress Control Number: 2022936662

ISBN: 978-1-63045-092-2

Music for Ghosts

For those who continued in spite of.

CONTENTS

Part I:

The Salvation Class

Part II:

To What Home

Part III:

Music for Ghosts

Music for Ghosts

What is it like
to come to, nowhere, in darkness
not knowing who you are, not
caring if the wind calms, the stars
stall in their sudden orbits,
the cities below go on without
you, screaming and singing?

—Philip Levine, "Scouting"

We can't remember our sins here. We don't know who we used to be.

—Denis Johnson, "The Stars at Noon"

The Only One

It is not enough to be lonely, or
alone. Though I am. Not enough
to stand in front of a second story
window blown open in June, perfumed
wrists of small lilac grubbing up
through daylight thrummed sticky
and green, brief winds carrying
a judgment of sweetness—proboscis
and honey as the flowers ooze complaints
from their many licked ears. Not enough
to commiserate, complain about lock
down in phone calls with my brothers
and my parents, but not my sister,
someone I refuse to this day, her life
tangled in deceit and rage, another
silence to add in my continuing orchestra
of loss. And it can't be enough to have
my youngest daughter weep in my arms
last night that she's afraid I don't love
her anymore, that her sister is the only
one I notice. Nothing to be said but
sweetheart, no, no, no, until she finally
quiets, and then stills, and the whole of
our house leans into the glittering dark.

Part I:
The Salvation Class

The Arsonist

This morning, I am naked under
cotton sheets, satiated and pleading
with no one, all the breaking sunrise
falling pink in the doorway like a Japan's
worth of blossom. It is this turmoil
of easy living, my life exempt from
the ruin I once prized, once felt
sweeping through me like the midnight
hands of a clock. How I sometimes
long for those days again; so much
blind rejoicing: stoned on oxys,
my hands on the steering wheel
and driving into the maw of some
luxurious nowhere, shirt pocket
blessed with twenty more, enough
to get me to Tuesday, as my daughters
waited for me back home, obediently
stacking themselves atop a pyre
I built, their love no match for fire.

Birds Without Music

5,000 red-winged blackbirds
rain unbidden from an Arkansas
sky like trench coats shot to pieces,
streets and lawns ankle-deep in little
bodies. A white-crested laughing
thrush bloated under a scrim of waste
water at the Miami Zoo, its black
streak across the eyes like an homage
to Annie Lenox until I reconsider,
sure God isn't a fan. The Baltimore
oriole with its head blown out, my brother
trembling as he tossed the pellet gun
into the rosebush and ran. The barn
swallow practicing his cursive until
my picture window, thud knocking
my attention away from the television
where a U shaped throng of republicans
ruffled themselves with speeches
on terror. And you, silent
on the long flight home
to America, news of your brother's
death only hours old, and how the night
before you said you wished to be
a starling, because starlings sing
for hours, sometimes longer.

East Wing

A nurse studies for finals past
midnight, small cone of light
elucidating the Latin words for
suffering. Next door, Mrs. Williams
is stretched out in a beautiful gondola
of morphine, gliding over the sunken
disasters to which she's attached her
pain. Her children couldn't deal so
they returned to a Motel 6 and said
their goodnights, the oldest knees
to chin in the tub, remembering
how panic once owned her beneath
the Paris streets. Lost in the catacombs,
she held a Bic lighter for her and her
mother, the flame unwrapping a row
of skulls bricked in the darkness, eye
sockets tunneling into some void they
could feel themselves collapsing: a legion
of fibula and metatarsal; breadbaskets
of sacrum and pelvis winged between
the shadows, her mother undone by all
the wreckage. "Your father didn't know
it was wrong," she said. "Besides,
you were too young to remember it."
And amazed, the daughter stared
at her mother amongst all those bones

and dreamed her escape, away from
those other terrors they could never
admit, or share. And the nurse now
stands and smooths her pleats, Mrs.
Williams pushing the bell. But not
because she is in pain or needs a drink,
or because she wants to know where
all her children have gone, but because
she wants to hear someone say her name,
to have it fill the air like an act of faith.

Looking Out A Window, I Am Reminded There Are Two Ways To See A Mountain

I like how Whiteface Mountain shoulders
a raincloud; it makes me happy enough
to forgive you. But then the clapping
of a large Japanese family in the dining
room reminds me dreams have no place
at work, so I open more bottles of wine
as the family tip their heads like sunflowers
for the guest of honor: a 90-year-old who
survived Guadalcanal. He smiles and raises
his hand and his wife cries across the table.
They all sing a song in Japanese and everyone
claps again and I feel more foreign than usual
even though I hear my chef yelling he's sick
of watching his food die beneath the heat
lamps. The bartender's drunk again and I
smile as his clumsy olives teeter into fogged
glasses and drink straws sliver the mahogany,
wet and abandoned. The old man stands up
and recites a poem by Basho, the one about
great soldiers and how summer grasses
are all that remain of their dreams, and I
understand, and want him to reveal what
that last night was like: the mud and the stench,
the blood a river in search of a name, but
know better than to interrupt, to embrace
a man lost in what it was that saved him.

Fox Luck

Humidity surprises the Adirondacks,
undaunted though this pod of bikers
barreling past my house; a Lycra procession
bright as poisonous frogs. But me, on my
hands and knees planting tomatoes, a stupor
of basil in little green rows. I stand and brush
the soil crumpled from my jeans, squint
and wave the midges face-free. This would
normally mean one beer then two. A third
feet up and splayed on the front porch. I'd
admire the twisting sky, the way heat colors
the clouds like blood filling a syringe. Then
early evening with its strange perfumes and
flowers trembled into shadow. I'd crack
number four while searing meat, cast iron
smoking like summer pavement. Number
five around the dinner table, the usual
questions of how was your day, dad, how
was your day. The couch with number six
as my children begin their long climb to bed,
the stories I don't tell of heroes and nymphs,
a rain of stars. But instead today I chug
the garden hose, wipe my mouth. I take
a long cool shower and close my eyes.
Then a quiet porch and present dinner.
At bedtime, I skooch between my girls
and describe brave oceans, warrior crows,
a magic trumpet that forgives its player
of every wrong choice. As finale, I explain
a fox has taken to visiting our garden, and in

the coiled dark, box fan tumbling moonlight
onto the bed, I say he's merely looking
for something he's lost, the soft arrow
head of his face gentle between
the tomatoes as he sniffs and moves,
separating dark from bush, bush from light.

Targets

He lifts his cellphone higher and waves
like Prospero assembling the clouds—
still no reception. Even here, a rest stop
glutted in New Jersey accents and head
lights dreaming every deer extinct. Others
simply leave: a van costumed in boys
ready for soccer or some other bloodless
parade; big rigs souped up on grit and
a week's worth of amphetamines. All
merge, untethering like fevered pearls
into a parkway tiled by lights creeping
north. But he has bigger fish to fry,
regrets leaving this morning before
she could decide; her shower hissed
behind the door as he pressed his ear
jealous for answers. So now he stretches
on his toes wishing he chose a different
carrier, that commercial with the salesgirl
both beautiful and vacant, like how he
feels right now, minus the beautiful
part. And as he waves again, halfway
frenetic, a stranger next to a Coke machine,
a man also wounded by the curse of dumb
choices, waves back, unsure, thinking
maybe it's that boy he couldn't love all
those years ago. And when he feels
something catch in his throat he waves
bigger, convinced, and that's when he

sees the phone, hears it ring as the man
pulls it to his mouth repeating a girl's name.
The stranger unsmiles and turns back toward
the lot. He worries he forgot to lock his car:
another easy target. And all the heartbreak after.

Billy Collins

August morning still cool, before
the sun ignites like an animal running.
And I lie in bed reading poem after
poem, a poet I once loved so much
I believed he alone could save me, never
mind I was near dead, my brother and I
in love with the idea of a single pill, then
ten, then a hundred, and finally a kingdom
of blue narcotics so high our voices
scraped the surface raw. I now close
the book, watch sunlight spider up the bed
room walls, and understand what I liked
about these poems: the repetition, the agreement
we'd reside in a world safe with Irish cows,
white clouds and history lessons, and the
occasional stalk of just-picked asparagus.

Torn

Right leg body bagged across
the coffee table, heavy as a marble
slab The Renaissance forgot. Sit
up and painful glug of knee;
the meniscus a dry 'O' like your
kiss before Chapstick. The femur
hi-fives the tibia under a thick
pudge of fluid; a snow globe
I try not to shake. Prescription
for Vicodin goes unheeded
at the pharmacy, its absence
now saving me. What's left
but a glass of cool water and the
stupor of Netflix, dusk pressing
the windows until they bruise.

Allegory

April 14, 2020

A blackbird's trapped inside my bedroom,
popping the bright window like a child's
gloved hand. Golden eyes eerie with pupils—
all of him nerve-wracked & wired & furiously
mute. I want what he wants, so I bend & creep
to the other window, grit-toothed & pillow
shielded, alive with Hitchcockian terrors I still
imagine, even at this age. I fumble with the sash,
look over my shoulder at another dry flourish,
his desire heated to almost a reckoning, & I
duck & weave & grimace until the frame
gapes & he funnels like chimney smoke up
into all that blue. But I never think to ask
where did he come from, & how did he choose
the silence of this house, this captive place
where we still dream lost as those wings.

Humiliation

April returns, and you
find yourself lost under
mountain pine, gin-tipped
pikes shagged green and harmless.
A recitation of loneliness, lips
counting the rings of headless
old growth. God fills the clouds
with his absence, boughs
steeped above you in halting
crush, unreachable as the corn
flower sky ringing with your bargain
at forgiveness, acceptance;
the ache of a cold bloom.

Eight New Ways Of Looking

—apologies to Wallace Stevens

The poem did not offer redemption
or even one blackbird, but still
you cried. You always cry. *Baby.*

The poem held its breath like
a diamond, but none of us
felt richer in its shine.

The poem said it was hungry,
and spread before us a banquet
of many shattered bowls.

The poem's jealous accusations
unbuttoned former lovers in
light carved from failure.

The poem was aroused
but silent, night filling your
mouth wet with darkness.

The poem needed its walker,
so you pushed it down the stairs.

The poem said it was thirsty
and I watched you open your veins.

The poem said the universe turns
in this handful of pills, releasing
a new weather inside me.

Waiting For The End Of The World

You may see them drowning as you stroll along the beach
But don't throw out the lifeline till they're clean out of reach
—Elvis Costello

Before 2012, preppers feared
the Mayan calendar and stocked jugs
of water, batteries, flashlights, cans
of soup stacked like cheap Warhols.
And then they entered their bunkers
until their wives told them
to come out. Others laughed
at the date, some ignored it. Hollywood
even made a terrible movie. And
how did you prepare besides sleep
with an intern as your wife
flew across the country embalmed
in Xanax? But don't worry,
two minutes after touchdown,
your wife's boyfriend was waiting
with the other onlookers, making
out the faces of the disembarked,
wondering, *Is that her? Is that?*
Flowers behind his back, a poem
he memorized about fate; eternity.

History Lesson

I start a fire good and fast
with birchbark, scouring darkness
from the walls. The iron stove
plumps like a vein, its little
window beating orange against
my face. It feels good driving
out the echo of last night; shouts
leaving exit wounds until our
daughter slammed her door
like a book of terrible endings.
I stand in a crackle of knees
and think October's taken liberties
too, pressed its cold cheek against
this house like a drunk uncle dancing
too close. It's left the trees humiliated,
their cadmium gowns snipped
into useless piles beneath them. I feel
equally naked and shamed. The heat
builds and I add more wood, brightness
the only rule I cannot break.

What The Dead Know

There are not enough pleasures
to simplify the spirit.
                    —*Charlie Smith*

The dead do not visit me at night; at 3 a.m.,
they do not glide over my bed to reveal a
mortal prophecy: "Avoid the morning train,"
or "A fire awaits you at the bakery." Nothing.
Just me split and pulled from the char

of a receding dream, alone in my sheets as night
counts the insomniac stars, the neighborhood
crushed in heaps of silence as no dog unravels
on its chain, no loitering Camaro sprays *Van Halen*
against our petrified boxwood. How can the dead

know I would prefer their blank company, their insolent
calm to all this ordinary nothing clogging the avenues
of sleep as I lie here and think of my stepfather
and how almost every night he sees whole lines
of the dead enter his room as if taking numbers, closing

in on him, telling him they await not in fire but in silence,
and he will be addition by subtraction, and that they
will lift him up to the others breathing behind the clouds
in their melancholy and their robes, lift him by the wrists
as if he were just cut down from some holy machine.

Counting

My daughter Grace has a weakness
for crows, points to one hopping the lid
of the café dumpster, its shoulders oiled
black as Elvis' pomp. And when we drive
home, two crows tightrope the highway's
yellow line, tap a squirrel pressed dry
as a flower. Even as I speed past they
are fearless, pompous struts like federal
judges before they sentence you to life.
I will release my crows on an unsuspecting
world and they will do my bidding, Grace
says. And I laugh, imagine a wide cape
of darkening sky as they fan out behind
her in a staccato of barks and cries. Home,
the car ticks in the driveway as I stand
in the yard, spy three adjourned in a sugar
maple: silent, disapproving, their languorous
stares unsure if they've noticed my face before.
Grace startles me from behind, places a silver
necklace in my hand. Leave it on the stump,
she says, so they'll know it's theirs. And
when I look back up, there are now four.

Part II:
To What Home

Autobiography Of The Table & The Kitchen

There have been meals I've loathed and meals
I've despised. Most recent, a rubbered patty
oozing beneath its own greased shambles at a
truck stop in Buffalo, the steam of plate-clatter
and diesel smoke the only things divine. Meals
eaten in silence when I was seven and the air
between my parents suffocated the table; doom's
easy smolder ready to fill our lives with smoke.
Meals joyous at drive-ins slicked in ketchup and
glazed napkins. Meals of befuddlement slung
mornings after childhood sleepovers, words
like *bagel* and *omelet* birthing a new lexicon
to mouth water. Meals of *Out! Out!* wooden
spoon cracking the pot's rim as children scattered
from the kitchen—giggling snipes. Meals of despair
before college, one room tenement as I jawed microwave
burritos stoned in my conviction the mattress bloomed
a Rorschach of clues. Meals of first dates palpitated
by whicker Chianti and the shedding of garments,
laughing about too much garlic as the sheets roiled
in our new hunger. Meals tilled from farmers markets
and roadside stands, Swiss chard a study in rare
plumage; waxy peppers shined like the tongues
of small fires. Solo meals of comfort after personal
disasters, the counter serving as respite for the maligned.
Meals of regret and meals of plenty. Meals
of family faces ensconced around a tablecloth
saved crisp just for meals like that. And meals

with you, simple across the table, all those years of
what we've said and what we couldn't. Meals best
enjoyed with our eyes instead of our stomachs, meals
when we couldn't fill our mouths fast enough. The meal
we had at a busted kitchen table in our new apartment
25 years ago, surprising you first with purple irises,
bottle of *Cote du Rhone* hollowed dry, the way you
stared at me, and me at your working mouth, your hair
swooning against your collarbones with a rhythm
I had grown to love, and me finally putting down
the fork and the knife, and lifting the napkin from
my lap, and coming over to you and raising us up
to the many-toothed stars and all their crying out.

A Christmas Story

Christmas Eve, street cloaked in the halogen fall of snow-
light. Curled beside me, my wife's arms around her stomach
as if they're the final levee. Gray, her face the cold mirrors
know. *I can't stop shaking*, she says. Flu. Infection. Or worse.
Wrapping presents, we'd been fighting moments before,
both of us so hurt we couldn't find language to assemble
the years. No choice now but to haul our daughters up from
the sticky depths they'd succumbed, happiness replaced
by the freezing upholstery of a backseat. We plow through
antiseptic drifts until a hospital rises from the storm & dark-
ness. Nurses reach in a ballet of white. Childish gown & a
disharmony of wires; waiting room where our children slump
heads as if recently betwinned. Doctor explains the need
for a specialist. The heavy whump of ambulance doors & my
wife is taken away. *Go home*, he tells me. *Get some rest.* Nothing
left but a silent drive back, my children returning to bed,
& me cross-armed in the living room amongst an obscenity
of gifts. I consider the tree's corset of lights, the handmade
ornaments: baby pictures glued between popsicle sticks, corn
husk woven into the body of an angel.

February in Salt Minor

Snowplows bring their gray news just
like the ocean waves outside our window,
morning walks always a puzzle of refuse
flung from the Atlantic's bayed vaults:

lobster traps sullen in their green crush
of wire voiceless against the shore; painted
buoys stiff on the sand like rockets out
of breath. We fill our pockets with beach

stones and let our thighs grow numb
with such frigid persistence, a coldness
rehearsed like our own: the burn of it,
the way ice leaches until all we've left

is stark enough to light a thousand arctic
suns, white and heavy as blindness.

Porcupine

> We trained
the headlights against its prehistoric,
nubbled shape and waited for it to cross
the road, rain a misery of *forgive me* down
our windshield, me still unsure who needed
absolution: us or some recent past.

> Almost there,
lumbering yet cautious, blue recycling
bin tipped empty on its side, wind
ringing the chokeberry in the adjacent
yard of a neighbor we haven't met,
three weeks since moving here to Maine;
long parchments of seaweed line our shore
like maps discerning where we've been,
where we hope never to return.

> The porcupine
finally passed, and when my daughter
wondered out loud if something helped
guide it, I imagined a mouse as crossing
guard, small sign gripped in his hand,
one of those bright orange vests made
by someone who loves him, who needs
the world to see him clearly in this rain.

Happy

But there are no happy endings, because if things are happy,
they have not ended.
　　　　　　　　—Donald Hall

Portland museum, slight chips of snow
ghosting the windows like ash off
cigarettes; a Maine sky imprisoned
with all the tough angels. We sit in
the building's belly, a café seizured

in beautiful pastries, croissants glazed
like tearful cheeks; popcorn labeled
as non-GMO and therefore, somehow,
healthy. We eat in silence, and I'm thinking
about the Pissarro on the third floor, and

that strange video tower being the only
piece which read "Please Touch", itchy
guards swimming the rooms with hope
you'd drag a finger down a Wyeth
so as to give them a reason. The girls

pipe up, start comparing the best key
lime pies they've ever had, the best
scones: "Nothing spongy," Grace says.
Sophie nods in agreement, mouth full.
My wife offers "What if we opened

a restaurant and called the kid's meal
a 'Happier Meal'," and it's my first
genuine laugh of the day. "That's
great," I say. "What would we serve?"
My wife shrugs, noncommittal.
And the nicest exchange we've
shared in days ends as quickly as
as it started, so we turn back
to our daughters, their talk silly,
natural, and yes, almost happy.

Orion In July

The lawns grow insane
with thirst, twisted rankles
reaching past the air and into
the mordant light, the sweet
haul of wood smoke and burning
fat conspire above my neighbor's
fence, the Marlboro bitten
between his teeth so his words
stay put. His mind turns like the meat
on the grill and he decides not to kill
his wife. All of us here are like that:
torn, slightly broken of charm and
insufferable in private ways we don't
know spells the end. But we pretend
to know better, and snap our chairs
onto the black squares of sidewalk
to watch the Harleys belch past us
into a world stripped of humor and clean
laundry, nights like the sound rust makes
in old men's throats, complaints
as sagged as the mattresses we bully
onto our roofs to escape the heat,
half alive, stars a blizzard doing
nothing and there's me, looking up,
still trying to find some god's belt.

Outside Limerick

From the train these hills look
like covered bodies, blanched
and indifferent, until a grey tunnel
of peat smoke wraps itself around
trees you'll never climb, let alone
touch, as a pair of starlings swoop
and fall like crumbs from a table. And
then someone's castle, as if on cue,
muscles into the picture, all stone and
varicose ivy as you try to remember
what it felt like to be held by someone
lacking an agenda: the woman in last
night's pub spinning a web of vodka
and asking if you wanted to crawl inside.

A young German couple in front of you,
chatty the whole ride, slip in one ear bud
apiece, smiling, grooving to nothing too
Wagner, maybe Top 40, and she closes
her eyes, charmed as a cobra, her only
concern maybe the hotel bed they left
this morning and how sad it is that now
all the sheets are cold. Or maybe it's
just you, wishing your own bed recalled
the urgency of thighs and stomachs pressed
hard enough to flush blood to the surface,
to fire, to the very tip of your aching tongue.

After The Fight

I felt empty as a cold chimney,
but walked through the rain
to a bridge, hands glazed
atop the railing, and listened
to the sideways pull of river-
murmur speak of someplace else,
somewhere our lives were less
than rumor. Back in the auditorium,
I drank water from a paper cup
the kind nurses hand you with pills.
My daughter was to go onstage, my
wife somewhere in the drop of house
lights. I paced the lobby. There were
doors all around me; I had to choose one.

Bible Study

Our bedroom in the basement, and the only
bathroom a creaking stairwell away, my brother
and I pissed late nights behind the washing
machine, bisecting damp cement from black
rubber tubing. Maybe we hoped a Maytag
could disinfect our awkward sizzlings? Or
maybe it was the fear of demons tongue
dripping in the darkness if we attempted
otherwise. Our church kept us in line,
testaments Satan would transform us
into compressed howlings if we didn't
always serve the Lord, didn't rebuke
sin through wild exaltations—a hymn
of arms lifting towards the ceiling lights in
showy obedience, like the way flowers rise
from their beds in April, bent and squinting,
unable to disregard the holy words of the sun.

Brothers

Exeter, NH 1985

The grapevine unraveling its sour
constellation, and chicken coop
collapsed like a lung. Our dog Ernie
waited out the last hen, feathers
erupting between his teeth. And I
can see my brothers standing near
the cellar door, one older and one
too young, goofing around or maybe
Josh running the bases in a Fenway Park
of the mind. We'd whack golf balls
into the woods until Brian grew curious
and tortured one open, rubber bands
popping and hissing against the flame.
We ran sputtering from the basement,
our family-strength mustard gas devouring
whole frogs in sadistic ritual. Not to mention
the pellet gun and songbirds knocked
from trees like warm fruit. We made fists
and pounded ourselves more senseless
than we already were until dad thought
it a good idea to don gloves and box
in the grass as Ernie barked and dad
served as a kind of benevolent referee.
We fired bottle rockets at clouds until
that got boring and so assaulted each
other, ducking and yelling *Wait! Stop!*

Not Fair! Year upon year stacked on itself
like dinner plates until we uprooted from
that yard and floated away like those balloons
we once set free, notes attached asking
whoever finds these please call this number,
the excitement of possibility, of adventure
we believed we were owed. The balloons
wobbled skyward, shrinking against
the sun, until they were harder to see,
until they were gone, and left were
three brothers looking up, each hoping
his life was about to begin.

Secrets

A father of two daughters, I do
not know the trial of sons, the spit
drool *Jump! Jump!* of sons; attacking
those who suggest their hearts
as braver, penis size, greater. I just
have two daughters: two soap
carved angelics unbuilt for war
or competition. Where, for no
good reason, one sister can turn
to the other and whisper a secret,
say something that has the power
to tear the other in half.

The Fifth of May

It seemed easy enough, the football
traveling from one pair of hands
to another, until I said go long,
the ball unzipping the air between
my daughter and me as she leapt,
eyes closed. This is where I break
her nose, I thought, but just like that
she hauled it in, more surprised than me.
Soft hands, I said. She smiled and chucked
it back, the ball tumbling like a shot duck,
which is an insult to ducks everywhere,
shot or otherwise. But neither of us cared,
and we managed a back and forth perfectly
suited for the day: the sky rinsed blue,
the garden freshly turned with new rows
of basil and rosemary, and the wind
content to lift our shouts and our cries into
a space more rarified than gratitude itself.

Heat Wave

Sun plucking sky like a sheet
music of bees, all of us hiding
in parlors and basements dug by
others long vanished. Humidity
sags between trees like church
bells underwater. No escape, no
amusement in the turkey sandwiches
stiffening atop plates, countertop
breadcrumbs a tiny Stonehenge
for ants dizzy at the offering. It is
not a day for creditors or salesmen;
a day with you on your hands and knees
in the garden like you've come
seeking forgiveness, nature rendered
sick and unbeautified. I cannot even
find solace in the quick dart of gold
finch, his back shamed yellow like
the sun—the original bully—as I stand
blinded in my yard, grass curling
beneath me like the toes of the dead.

Gather

When I was seven I worried about
my height, if I'd be tall enough
to reach the cereal box throned
above the kitchen sink, or shag
a baseball before it comet-tailed over
the fence. I could certainly pocket
the matches from the dining room table
and conjure smoke behind our neighbor's
garage, the fire raising its body higher
than any of us. And most days I could
lift my gaze to the ceiling and listen
as my parents argued above me about
whose sadness was more essential, their claims
so young and ruinous. But I'd grow bored
and look out the back window at the grape
vine gone feral against the chain link, my love
of popping those dusty globes between
my teeth, each cluster something I could
easily reach and claim as my own.

On Learning We Would Not Lose The House

The news dismantled sorrow; saved
us. Like the condemned sung free,
we rejoiced until raw and shouting,
danced the green from the lawn's
thick pelt. We were so loud we could
not hear the future, could not see
November or those deputies apologizing
from a doorway no longer ours, gray
ropes of sunshine wrung useless between
the telephone wires. For now, we only
knew this moment. Someone fired up
the grill as the children formed hunting
parties, entering the woods in a giggling
line. A bottle was passed from one adult
to another and dragonflies buttered
the air; one even traced my daughter's
shoulder before attaching to the back
of her head. And as I reached out to
touch it, I noticed it glowed smoky
pink, barely a cinder—not enough
heat to light even the fires of the poor.

Part III:
Music for Ghosts

Trues Ledge

Lebanon, NH

Its name incites hope, a chance
to lift this year's shadow, but your
dress shoes nearly falter, the trail
shattered in oak leaves, November
air so raw even the saplings bow
inconsolable. We stand at the rim,
a gorge perfect for young love to fling
itself over after nobody understands,
and I smile at the pageantry, thankful
I've forgotten such claims. I manage
my way down, careful in my footing
as I shake rainwater from young pine,
prickling my neck and my hair. I
discover a white sluice of roaring
channeled between rocks, unending,
mist rising like prayer until I spy you
above, looking down over what is left,
both truth and memory between us
and every landscape we've left behind.

Angels

Clouds stretch a blindfold grey
across the stars, and everything I've
learned about devotion sifts down
in endless flakes, tracing the angle
between you and your animal
breath, shovel parting the air like
beaded curtains. Grill and lawn chair
fill bright with emptiness, and you
watch the field grow deeper, where
last summer a trailer went up in flames,
and the mother broke free, herself on fire
as she made a path burning through
the milkweed and collapsed holding
a blue swaddle smoking like something
unholy, and which none of the rescuers
dared name. And for once everyone came
to the church, the white boards stacked
around the hum of their suffering as the pastor
reminded them they can't ever know His
plan, even as they lined up to say how
sorry they were to a man newly bewildered.
So now, with nothing to be done, you turn
back to your job of clearing driveway and
walkway, relieving the earth of weight so soft
children could collapse and make angels.

Rush

Defiant under clear threads
of rain, a girl hoists an umbrella
like a picket sign against gloom
and rubberboots down to the bus
stop. Behind, a carload of teens
play target practice, hitting one
pothole after another spraying fire
hydrant and mailbox. They pass
a joint like a sextant revealing
a way out of this life. The windows
dampen with smoke, cloud the hard
lines of jaw and Adams apple soft
enough to believe they are children,
because they are. The girl hears them
coming, a great trundled hissing, until
the driver yells "Bullseye!" and the girl
stands sodden, umbrella wilted, and one
of the boys stops laughing long enough
to catch his reflection in the mirror: beaming,
victorious. And it goes on like this block
by block, year by year; rushing toward
some ending they would never believe.

Brushstrokes

Finally it was night in *Sevilla*, the air
warm and tumbling past the gates
of our bodies, a wooden trellis stitched
with night-blooming jasmine, perfume
slunk dark and delicious. What starlight
there was chinked the river, small waves
opening near our feet like palms upturned,
and understanding want I plunked
a coin, one hundred *pesetas*, silver winking
until the river blackened my wish. We were
still wobbled from dinner: a busy courtyard,
long tables where locals hoisted beer, octopus
dripping oil, hazelnuts roasted brown
until they crunched like split wood; great
bolts of fabric strewn high above us, shade
against the daytime sun, insufferable,
unrepentant. We couldn't keep our hands
off each other, and paying the bill, slanted
ourselves down another alley, another table,
more *jamon y queso*, sherry chilled colder
than the winter we fled in New Hampshire,
its eaves now iced into rows of crystalline
teeth. You promised me body and marrow,
a mouth wet to the touch, reminding me
of the night we made love in your car
after the O'Keefe exhibit; all those
swollen iris and red poppy. And how
you made me taste every petal.

The Female Suicide Bomber Does Not Consider Young Love

Ankara, March 16, 2016

The black vest squeezes her ribs
until belief: chrysalis bursting
like a thousand siroccos de-
constructing bone from hair,
skin from breath, the siren's red
dervish striping cement and gritted
teeth; fractured rebar crumpled
into a wild begging. A first date
walked hand in hand moments
before, and they were both so joy
stricken they believed they could
leave this world and live amongst
the rain, the bread of clouds.

Late Return

Harmless really, the dog arthritic
      as icy rust, uncoiling fragile barks
at Sophie running out to see me before
      I drove off. I was trapped in my car,
the dog owner between us all sunflower
      and grandmotherly charm. So I
motioned, had to say *Please, your dog, my daughter…*
      And then the part I didn't want
to admit: *She was bitten before.*
      This new dog made Sophie freeze
tight as December maple, juiceless
      and heavy, and the owner smiled, telling
her, "It's okay, I have seven grand kids
      of my own," and took the dog away.
Yet in the car, unable to leave, shaking,
      repeating to Sophie I'm sorry, holding
her, I remembered the first time all those
      years ago: the way the dog disheveled
her, splashed her into the grass, tried to unSophie
      her, teeth locking in place like gears
oiled to their own need, and me too late
      to stop it; that stone I still carry.

Visitation

–for Sophie, age 8

Not the leg-sucking clam bed,
Sophie stuck up to her knees, tide out and rocks
gulping at their own nakedness.
                    Not the trails scraped in snowmelt
winding the nearby woods where she lost
her blue mitten as we spied deer prints
and coyote prints thinned to crystal relics.
                    Not the quick
slip to pavement, leg rubied in bright
scratches, lower lip quivering, incapable
of holding so many indignities in such short
order. No. It was Sophie uttering her desire,
limping now, to just once see an owl's face
"...in real life," until all of us stopped
in our boots on that wet country road
as one appeared, barred and mute
in the twilit branches above. We stared
a good, long time until *I* hooted, and the owl
lifted away into a deeper silence.
                    And there was Sophie,
shy again, walking upright, even as we returned
to the house where all the windows were dark.

Doubleback

Public library, I pick the edge of a suicide
hotline sticker and wonder who called.
Maybe he needed someone to know
his marriage was killing him: meek
orgasms alone in the shower. Nighttime
a reverie of silence as they lay back to back
thinking: *we're sticking it out for the kids.*
Or it was worse: reason an aperture
closing, a bullet like Solomon offering
compromise: divide temple from jaw if only
for the asking. What were his grievances
then? I look out the vaulted windows
and onto a lake held down by tire treads
and ice, remember as a boy how I trembled
at that shore until near darkness, hoping
tonight please not another negotiation,
please not mom crying at her empty hands
and dad long gone by dinner, please not this
gripping hold of loneliness I feel on me
every day as nothing no how no way
until prayers in bed dear lord I'm sorry
please forgive me I'm lost amen and amen.

Absolution

The way he holds you
back, hands boiling
with small bones spelling
desire. A push open; that
glittered thrum under breastbone
like blue jays clapping sunlight
from the pines. His knees
consider the weight of everything,
even what fills his mouth like
an offering to this life or the next,
night draining into night, until all
reason is reduced to the study
of a man's head in your hands,
and a sound like water: slow,
persistent—as if blessing your
name in a different tongue.

Repentance

Splayed across cement like a grim
Jesus, he bled through a hospital
gown too short to find his knees.
A woman held his face, crying
for God while two cops hovered
instead. You couldn't take any
of it and muscled to the escalator
with its slow baptism of light, exhaust
dying from your hair until a sudden
punch of street-wind as someone
laughed, clearly in love, cab door
shutting behind. The traffic pressed
tight as hands in supplication; those
days of your childhood when you believed
prayer could save anyone, even you.

Sacrament

Still I cannot reach you, you
of burnt tongue and predictable
need, intentions dull as gold
with the shine hammered out.
Just this morning you watched
beauty run its blast radius straight
to the Chesapeake, and hawks wheeled
as if God was cracking a blue safe.
But you were gone, or maybe never
there. What heart, you said. Where?
As the world continued undressing,
bleeding and dreaming without you.

So Emo

I want David Bowie to lead me up
from the turntable and into the streets
of Berlin. But instead, I concentrate on
the penny taped to the needle, its copper
weight an antidote to all the crackled
bouncing. I finish my fourth Michelob,
tucking the empty under my bed
with the others. My parents will
be home any minute and I've lost
all fear of them; what do they know—
not heartbreak paraded amongst
a wilderness of lockers, or the decry
of a football team mumbling
faggot as their fists pound invisible
spikes into my skull, my French
teacher turning thankfully away.
My eyes marvel the razor's bright
anthem: so much fresh canvas of leg
and arm and chest and the warm drip
of paint drying outback where I
graffitied a giant, circled "A"
for anarchy against the broke-down
chicken coop, letting people know
not to mess with me. I am supreme
ruler of this domain—this shuttered
room of overturned laundry and shameful
orgasms. I turn back to the music:
Bowie lilts and chunders and promises
we can all be heroes as my parents' car
cuts like a shark into the darkening drive.

Lake George

Jefferson proclaimed it the most
beautiful water, and high up on
this ridge, the aster and goldenrod
touching hands, we can see why:
it stretches blue over thirty miles,
islands like well-groomed heads
rising luxurious and clean. Sunlight
ghosts between the milkweed as my
two daughters complain they're thirsty,
ironic as most all we see is water.
Earlier, in the rock and roll sushi joint,
Gracie nibbled rice as if in a contest
to underwhelm, and I worried her
teenage years before me, asked if she
ever felt that food was an obstacle,
something she could prove wrong.
She shrugged her shoulders and sipped
green tea, and I understood we'd become
two trains blameless toward their own
horizons. It saddens me, and as we make
our way to the bottom of the hill, Sophie
discovers a pond burping with frogs.
She laughs and swoops them up, collects
them into a found bucket until Gracie shoos
them out, tells them to run away. And
as I try to intervene, console one and
admonish the other, I think I'm no
different, trying to legalize every

mistake that still holds me weightless,
circles my life like ashes around the moon.
But as I stand between them, hands apart,
I fear this is the moment they always
knew was coming, the day I must choose.

Trespassers

The snow, bread-torn and
scattered, patchworks this field
and this wood, this narrow chasm
through which the three of us falter.
My wife walks ahead as if in a different
movie, a silent picture that ends
with her arrival somewhere else,
radiant and alone, and its all I can
do not to wish her luck. Sophie
doesn't notice, or is kind enough
to pretend otherwise, and instead yanks
an adolescent maple down by its neck,
bounces its snowy crown to dust,
laughing. Her joy lengthens the distance
between us, compounds Gracie's absence;
it's been months since she joined these
hikes—*what did she call them?*—to nowhere.
Now she spends weekends with friends, my
fear she's repeating what I did at her
age: raiding liquor cabinets or agreeing
to the next great high, images of her
discovering new, beautiful countries
of loneliness. I chase Sophie uphill
then down, ice-weary and heaving,
dodging tiny snowballs made by tinier
hands. My wife leans against a spruce,
"Pull her close," she commands, so I do.
She snaps a photo with her phone, stores it
in a place I no longer have access, a border
I am no longer allowed to cross.

The Last Of The Open-Heart Astronomers

Mowing a dark sea
of lawn behind your home,
you sweat and shove the engine
like a raw-mouthed god, push it
churning above a great furnace
of yellow jackets until they are so
enraptured, so possessed, they burst
skyward and fan a tornado of cursing
debris. So you turn from your
machine, the grass, the cloud
of pain engulfing you with its
miniature complaints, and run
blind towards some other country,
one that only speaks in low, soft
tones, and you can't believe,
as your knees decide to pray,
that you've become this helpless,
this incapable, until they descend
on you like evening, and tired of
naming stars, you close your eyes.

Acknowledgments

I would like to thank the editors of the following magazines where some of these poems first appeared:

The Adirondack Review; Anomaly Literary Journal (London)*; Another Chicago Magazine; Audubon; Bare Hands Poetry* (Dublin); *Blueline; Canary; Dash; Gargoyle; Like Light: 25 Years of Poetry & Prose by Bright Hill Poets & Writers; The McNeese Review; Moon City Review; Mudlark; The Night Heron Barks; Noble/Gas Qtrly; Northern Cardinal Review; North American Review; The Portland Press Herald; RHINO; Saranac Review; Spillway, Tuck; Upstreet, Whiskey Island*

Big thanks to **The Authors League Fund** for much needed financial assistance during the completion of this book.

Christopher Locke was born in New Hampshire and received his MFA from Goddard College. His poems have appeared in, among others, *The North American Review, Another Chicago Magazine, Poetry East, Verse Daily, Southwest Review, The Literary Review, The Sun, West Branch, Rattle, 32 Poems, Rhino, Saranac Review, The Southeast Review,* and *The Adirondack Review.* He won the Dorothy Sargent Rosenberg Poetry Award, as well as grants in poetry from the Massachusetts Cultural Council and the New Hampshire State Council on the Arts. *25 Trumbulls Road,* his first collection of fiction, won the Black River Chapbook Award. His new collection of essays *Without Saints* (Black Lawrence Press) is due in 2022. Chris lives in the Adirondacks and teaches English at SUNY Plattsburgh and North Country Community College.